Original title:
The Sting of the Sea

Copyright © 2025 Creative Arts Management OÜ
All rights reserved.

Author: Samuel Kensington
ISBN HARDBACK: 978-1-80587-263-4
ISBN PAPERBACK: 978-1-80587-733-2

Harbingers of the Deep

Fish in tuxedos, oh what a sight,
They dance on the waves, such a goofy delight.
Octopuses juggle, all hands in the air,
Crabs with their sassy moves, no one can compare.

Jellyfish bouncing like pillows of fluff,
They float past the sailors, all giggles and puff.
Squids tell tall tales with ink as their glue,
While seagulls perform in a comical hue.

Blackened Horizons

The sun took a dip, turned the world a dark gray,
But starfish are laughing, come join in their play!
Shells spin like tops, wind whispers with glee,
As mermaids crack jokes beneath the old tree.

Pirates forgot maps, switched to games instead,
Playing cards with a dolphin, who deals from his head.
Waves chuckle softly, a slap on the back,
Boundless laughter echoes, as the ship takes a crack.

Twilight on a Marooned Isle

Coconuts chatter, their gossip unkind,
As palm trees sway in a rhythm aligned.
Monkey in sunglasses, he takes a bold leap,
Splashing in waters, with secrets to keep.

Crabs in a huddle, they start a debate,
Who's fastest on sand? They just can't wait.
The moon starts to giggle, a disco ball bright,
As creatures of night dance with pure delight.

Veins of the Ocean

Eels with their hairstyles defy all the trends,
As dolphins pick favorites among their best friends.
Coral reefs chuckle, vibrant and spry,
While fish do impressions that make them all cry.

The tides tell secrets, with burbles and bubbles,
A whale goes by singing, it's full of soft cuddles.
With currents that twist, they giggle and spin,
Life under the waves, where the fun never ends.

Glistening Traps

When waves wear their sparkly crowns,
Fish get caught without any frowns.
A slippery eel in a soap-like dance,
Laughing at hooks in a whimsical trance.

Seagulls squawk in a raucous glee,
While crabs conspire as clever as can be.
They snag their lunch and pull it away,
While swimmers just flounder, adding to the play.

Shadows of Driftwood

Driftwood smiles under the sun's warm beams,
Telling tall tales and grander dreams.
Seashells giggle, they've much to say,
As tides pull together a funny ballet.

Three-legged crabs with a limby routine,
Dance the cha-cha without ever seen.
With one little twist, and a great big flip,
They've turned the shoreline into a comic strip.

Whirlpools of Despair

A whirlpool swirls with comical fuss,
It pulls in flotsam—a very odd bus.
Fish in the back are enjoying the ride,
While sailors just hang on, swept in the tide.

Frogs in the front croak out a new tune,
As the current dances beneath the bright moon.
The ocean chuckles, a jovial tease,
While sea creatures swim with ridiculous ease.

Chasms of Solitude

In a chasm deep where echoes abound,
Lonely sea urchins turn round and round.
They sigh and they moan in a symphony sweet,
While bubbles burst forth in a silly repeat.

Starfish play poker, what a strange sight,
With cards made of kelp under soft silver light.
They laugh at the waves, so bold and grand,
As trippy fish join in, taking a stand.

Venomous Currents

The jellyfish danced with a grin,
While seagulls squawked, playing the violin.
A crab waved its claws, oh what a show!
With each wavering move, it stole the flow.

A fish in a tuxedo tried to prance,
But slipped on seaweed, lost its chance.
A dolphin chuckled, flipped in delight,
As the wave swept the fish out of sight.

The Tempest's Caress

The wind whistled tunes that made you smile,
As waves stretched the ocean's playful style.
A pirate parrot flapped with flair,
While swabbing the deck without a care.

Lightning flashed like a zany spark,
As thunder giggled, leaving its mark.
Majestic whales strutted side to side,
Creating a splash with every wild ride.

Secrets of the Ocean's Heart

A clam told tales, witty and sly,
Of barnacles knitting, oh my, oh my!
Starfish laughed, sharing secrets so bright,
With a wink and a nudge in the shimmering light.

The seaweed swayed, a fashionable trend,
While crabs held a party, oh what a blend!
They danced on the sand, with a funny little twist,
In a frothy uproar, who could resist?

Lurking in the Brine

A shark wore glasses, felt rather cool,
As it floated by, breaking all the rules.
A turtle wore sneakers, so spry and keen,
Competing in races, oh what a scene!

The sea cucumbers grooved with ease,
While fish formed a chorus, ready to tease.
With bubbles and giggles, the ocean would cheer,
For the wild dance party of every sea year!

Conundrum of the Coasts

A crab in a top hat, quite dapper,
Struts down the beach, not caring a snapper.
He orders a soda with a twist of lime,
While seagulls debate the best way to mime.

The waves whisper secrets, oh what a tease,
A fish in a tux dreams of swimming with ease.
Seashells giggle, collecting the sand,
As octopuses ponder a band to command.

Drowning in Deception

A fish tells a tale of a diver's big blunder,
While dolphins all laugh, creating the thunder.
'He thought he could swim with a slice of bread,
But forgot that his lunch is not meant for his head!'

Giant squids nod, while snug in their lairs,
'Next time show up with a few more cares!
Who knew the ocean was so full of jest?
Here's hoping he learns, 'cause we've all been a pest!'

Blood on the Coral Reef

Anemones dance with festive delight,
While clowns in the waves turn day into night.
But a shark dressed as Cupid, oh what a fright,
Mistakes a big fish for a romantic sight!

Coral blooms blush as they watch the charade,
While mollusks and crabs join the parade.
A ballet of bubbles, the ocean's grand show,
With everyone laughing at the jokes down below.

The Ocean's Silent Wrath

The tides hold a secret, a chuckle or two,
As whales pull pranks on the boats sailing through.
'Those fishermen think they're the kings of the sea,'
But the seaweed all snickers—'Oh please, can't you see?'

With a splash and a flick, they divert their grand haul,
And sea cucumbers giggle in the briny sprawl.
If laughter's a treasure, the ocean's a chest,
In the depths of the blue, we find humor's best jest!

Sirens of the Forgotten

Underwater giggles lure the brave,
A fish dressed in pearls, a treasure knave.
Flipping fins and making waves,
Their laughter echoes, the ocean saves.

A crab does the cha-cha on the sand,
With clamshells clapping, it's quite a band.
A jellyfish dances, swaying free,
While seagulls squawk, 'What a sight to see!'

Coral castles made of creamy pie,
Starfish jesters, oh my, oh my!
In seaweed wigs, the mermaids prance,
Holding shells, they lead a merry dance.

So if you dive, beware the tease,
The charm of the depths can tickle with ease.
For in the blue where laughter reigns,
The quirks of the tide will surely entertain.

Battered Dreams

Waves toss in a wild caper,
A lost flip-flop is now a draper.
Seagulls steal your beachside lunch,
As surfboards clash in a hungry crunch.

Bikini tops and shorts in flight,
A sudden squall brings quite a fright.
With ice cream melting on the sand,
We chase the scoop, now out of hand.

The ocean bed is a laundry space,
Where socks and towels find their place.
A pirate's hat gets swirled away,
Next to a duck with a belly sway.

Yet smiles shine through the salty air,
With giggles bouncing everywhere.
Despite the mess, we hold our dreams,
In golden laughter, life redeems.

Castaway Whispers

A castaway with briny hair,
Sings to the gulls without a care.
His coconut cup spills a drink,
As crabs gather for a merry link.

You'd think he's lost, but he's quite sound,
With flip-flops made of beach foam found.
He trades tall tales with the tide,
In every wave, his woes subside.

His pet, a turtle, wears a hat,
While finding snacks from a nearby mat.
They catch the sun while others swim,
In ragged shorts that look quite grim.

As sunsets paint the sky with glee,
He taps his foot to the ocean's spree.
For on this shore, with laughter and cheer,
The whispers of joy are all we hear.

Silenced by the Surf

The sea sings soft, a comic tune,
With barnacle barbers, it's quite a boon.
Sea cucumbers with rolling eyes,
Complain about fish and silly lies.

A dolphin jokes with flip and splash,
While octopus arms make a colorful stash.
The seaweed sways with a giggly twist,
As shells giggle, 'Don't be missed!'

Sandcastles fall with a splat and thud,
Waves whisper secrets in bubbly flood.
Sea horses trot in ridiculous dress,
While crabs in bow ties cause quite a mess.

Yet amidst the chaos, joy takes its helm,
On shores where laughter, like water, overwhelm.
For in this place of frolic and fun,
Life's a beach, and we all are one.

Aqueous Betrayal

Bubbles rise and fish swim fast,
Jellyfish float, but oh, so brash.
With tentacles long, they wave goodbye,
Their slippery dance makes sailors cry.

Caught in a net of salty glee,
The ocean's prank, it's plain to see.
One moment you're high, the next you're low,
Who knew a splash could steal the show?

Siren's Sharp Embrace

A mermaid giggles, her hair a mess,
With scales that glisten, who'd ever guess?
She pulls you close with a wink and a pucker,
But watch your toes, she's no kind of plucker!

Her fishy friends offer a clownish grin,
As they plot to tickle you under your chin.
But when you're wrapped in her watery hug,
You'll find that laughter is all but snug.

Cursed Depths

Beneath the waves, where shadows creep,
A grumpy crab with a secret to keep.
He grumbles and mutters, his claws in a twist,
Making all sailors think they've been kissed!

Dancing octopuses spill ink in delight,
As sardines parade in glittering flight.
But beware the depths where laughter turns sour,
The ticklish eel holds a shocking power.

Undercurrents of Pain

The tide rolls in with a mischievous sway,
And seaweed giggles as it leads you astray.
You try to take a dip, but oh what a plight,
You wrestle with waves that just want to bite!

From sandcastles crumbled, to fishy foul play,
The ocean's a court, and it's court jesters' day.
So laugh with the tides and dance with the spray,
For under the surface, it's all just a play!

Coral's Veil

In hues of pink, the corals sway,
A fish in disguise, lost in the fray.
With laughter loud, they do a dance,
A jellyfish, awkward in its prance.

Bubbles burst as crabs applaud,
While sea turtles jog, a bit flawed.
A seagull squawks with a cheeky grin,
In this watery circus, let fun begin!

Anemones wave like fluffy hands,
Tickled by currents, making plans.
With quirky friends, they play all day,
In a splashy parade, come join the way!

So beneath the waves, where laughter rings,
Fishes wear hats, and the octopus sings.
A jester's realm, in ocean's embrace,
Coral's veil wraps us in joyous grace.

Bitter Waters

A ship sets sail with a wobbly crew,
Each sailor bold with a sip or two.
The horizon clear, yet stomachs churn,
With salty tales that twist and turn.

Nautical knots tied with spaghetti strands,
Fishes poke fun at the haphazard hands.
A parrot squawks, 'What a fabulous mess!'
As the captain's hat lands on an octopus's chest.

A corkscrew wave, a dizzying flight,
Mermaids chuckle at their wild plight.
But in this whirl of mishaps and dreams,
Is a world of laughter bursting at the seams!

Through waters bitter, yet filled with glee,
Every splash is a giggle, can't you see?
So let's toast to blunders, raise our glass,
In salty chaos, may our joy never pass!

Pirates of the Pained Coast

Ahoy, matey! With an eye of glass,
A pirate sneezes—'tis a sticky mass!
With rum-laden dreams and tales of yore,
Their ship's a circus, can't take much more!

They search for treasure but find a shoe,
One swabs the deck while others strew.
And in between the giggles and yells,
The ghostly sea captain spins yarns and dells.

Each cannon blast is a loud surprise,
As parrots squawk like snarky spies.
With swords that wobble, and hats askew,
Our jolly crew is all askew!

They dance on the plank, whoops, down they go!
In a splash of the waves, what a grand show!
So raise up the flag, let your laughter boast,
For these wacky pirates love their toast!

The Sorrowful Undertow

Beneath the waves, where giggles fade,
An undertow pulls, but it's all a charade.
With fish in bow ties and crabs in shoes,
They swim in circles, spreading their blues.

A sea cucumber sighs, 'What a day indeed,'
While plankton throws a party, feeling freed.
Jellyfish waltz with a ghostly grace,
Whispers of laughter in this watery space.

But the mermaids chuckle, tangled in hair,
They've misplaced their combs, oh, such a scare!
They splash and giggle, whilst trying to work,
In this sorrowful dance, the fun has its perk.

So raise your fin high, and embrace the flow,
In the undertow's clutch, let the giggles grow.
For through every wave, in currents that bend,
There lies a joke, and laughter's our friend!

Tranquil Deception

On gently rippling waves, they glide,
With fishy smiles, they all abide.
The seagulls squawk, a raucous jest,
While barnacles play host to the best.

As nets come down with a clatter,
The laughter fades, oh, what a matter!
The shrimp, they prance, trying to flee,
While crabs prepare for their own jubilee.

Oh what a show, the ocean's stage,
Where every splash turns the page.
With belly laughs from fishy folks,
They dance and twist, sharing jokes.

But when hook and line start to twirl,
The clowns become a dizzy whirl.
A circus act beneath the brine,
Where gimmicks live and fishers dine.

Beneath the Salted Foam

Beneath the waves, a tale unfolds,
Of fishy tricks and tales retold.
The octopus sports a silly hat,
While dolphins giggle at a flat.

A crab pulls pranks, his eyes all wide,
He skitters left, then slips aside.
Fish flail about in a comical dance,
Oblivious to the line of chance.

Splashing and crashing, a bubbly spree,
Where every wave holds a new decree.
But watch out, friends, for a sneaky bite,
You'll never see it coming, not one sight!

So laugh and swim, and take your time,
For nature's humor is truly prime.
In the ocean's joke, the punchline's clear,
What ghosts are lurking, we all can fear!

Lament of the Drowned

In gurgled murmurs, the sea creatures sigh,
While drowned men's boots mark stories nearby.
They tell of snacks gone totally wrong,
As they start to echo a funny song.

One fish bemoans his lost, crunchy chip,
While clams toss back with a salty quip.
From the deep blue yonder, a valiant plea,
"Spare us the hooks! We just want some tea!"

Eels twine together, slapping their tails,
As squid shoot ink and launch little fails.
The gales whistle loud, stealing the chance,
For a jolly good laugh amidst ocean's dance.

Yet still there lingers an odd little tale,
Of treasure lost and ships set to sail.
With bubbles and giggles, the tangle of woe,
The drowned's lament is a slapstick show!

Depths of Betrayal

In the briny depths where mischief reigns,
The fish can't trust the octopus's chains.
Allies today, enemies tomorrow,
As seaweed tugs at a spine of sorrow.

The pufferfish boasts of his swanky flair,
But friends gather 'round and start to stare.
"Don't let him lead you down to the gloom,
His party tricks lead to doom and gloom!"

The jellyfish floats with deceptive grace,
Whispering secrets in a silent place.
While clownfish giggle, plotting their pranks,
The ocean's underbelly is filled with thanks.

So watch your back in the salty tide,
For humor and treachery often collide.
In the murky depths, the laughter will flow,
Just as surely as the tides will show!

The Depth's Unkindness

In ocean's belly, fish do pout,
They swim with sadness, no doubt about.
A crab with claws, a wink so sly,
As munching gulls float overhead, oh my!

An octopus wears a hat too tight,
He trips on his limbs in a comic plight.
With jellyfish friends, he dances and sways,
While salty sea dogs just grumble and gaze.

The Ocean's Veil

Beneath the waves, a party's on,
Where fish don't care if they've got it wrong.
Seahorses twirl in silly attire,
While turtles snooze, they couldn't be higher.

A dolphin cracks jokes, there's laughter all day,
As crabs tell tales in a comedic way.
The seaweed wiggles, a green curly wig,
And starfish applaud, oh, they giggle big!

Secrets in the Swell

The swell whispers secrets, but they're just fish tales,
Like how the clam won at bingo, with big shiny scales.
A mermaid with glitter, oh, she loves to primp,
While seals breakdance, giving the waves a limp.

The mackerel boast with their shimmery flair,
While sardines huddle, in quite a scare.
Anemones chuckle, they wiggle around,
In the world below, joy can abound.

Tribulations of the Tide

The tide comes in with a splashing sound,
Crabs take cover, scuttling around.
A fish in a tux, what a sight to see,
Stumbles and tumbles, oh, how could it be?

With every wave, a splashy surprise,
Seagulls are cackling, rolling their eyes.
Some fish are swooning, in a little ballet,
As waves throw a party, come join the fray!

Abyssal Encounters

A fish in a suit, quite absurdly dressed,
Tried to sell me seashells, who'd have guessed?
It wiggled and jiggled, slick as could be,
I laughed so hard, nearly fell in the sea.

A crab with a grin, on a surfboard did ride,
Claiming he's king, with nothing to hide.
He winked and I chuckled, just can't take a chance,
He turned and he danced, in a sideways prance.

A dolphin in bowtie, tried his best to woo,
With a leap and a spin, he fell right in blue.
I rolled on the sand, in this wild melee,
Who knew the ocean could throw such a play?

A seaweed brigade, they started a band,
With a jellyfish drummer who danced like a hand.
They grooved to the rhythm of waves all around,
In this funky ocean, joy suddenly found.

Ripples of Regret

A mermaid in goggles swam by with a grin,
"Try my new sunscreen!" she called from within.
I took a small dab, thought I'd try something new,
Twelve hours later, I was bright shade of blue.

An octopus painter was splashing the tide,
He painted my arm, I just wanted to hide.
With polka dot patterns, I laughed at my fate,
Now I'm the ocean's most colorful mate!

A seagull named Gary, with style and such flair,
Said "Join me for brunch, there's krill in the air!"
But I took a wrong turn, ended up in a stew,
Now dinner's on me, and I just can't chew.

With clams and shrimp gossip, I sat by the shore,
Laughing at blunders that I can't ignore.
Each wave brought a chuckle, a splash and a cheer,
But every bright moment came with a sneer.

The Tempest's Caress

The wind howled a tune, like a jester at play,
As waves danced around in a hula ballet.
A sailor's lost hat flew high through the mist,
Towards seagulls who laughed at such perilous twist.

A lighthouse in dance, it swayed to and fro,
While ships tossed and turned like they didn't know.
In the chaos I giggled, on this wild ride,
The storm was our host, with nothing to hide.

A dolphin in trouble, he tried to keep pace,
With sea foam and bubbles, all over the place.
He jumped and he splashed, a most comical sight,
Making friends with the thunder, what a joyful fright!

The rain turned to giggles, the clouds wore a frown,
As thunder turned into a snort and a clown.
With laughter in torrents, we embraced the tide,
In this wild tempest where fun was a guide.

Fangs of the Four Winds

A shark on a surfboard, all teeth and no fear,
Told me he'd teach me to surf without fear!
He wiped out so hard, I can't hold my grin,
"Next time," he said, "I'll just stick to the fin!"

The gulls with their gossip, in shrieks and in squawks,
Clapped wings in delight, adding flair to the talks.
They swooped in to tease, with a sly little cheer,
As the shark shook it off, without any fear.

The tides tossed and tumbled with giggles and glee,
While crabs played tag, elusive as can be.
I joined in the laughter, we rolled with the beat,
In this ocean of jest, where joy's bittersweet.

The currents conspired like friends in a mess,
Each wave held a story, each splash was a jest.
We danced through the chaos, with mirth on display,
In a realm filled with laughter, we'd frolic and play.

Echoing Regrets

The fish swam past with a cheeky grin,
I thought I'd catch him, but where to begin?
My net got stuck on a seaweed snare,
Now it's a hat for a crab with flair.

I stood on the pier, feeling quite bold,
Dropped my sandwich, oh, the seagulls unfold!
They took to the skies, a feathered brigade,
My lunch turned to chaos, a lunchbox parade.

The waves made me think of my glorious fate,
But tossed by the surf, I was late for a date.
I laughed through the splashes, all soaked to the bone,
Turns out dinner's gone, with fish all alone.

I set out for treasures of shells and of pearls,
Instead, found a jellyfish dancing with swirls.
It stung like my jokes on a good friend's face,
I'll stick to dry land; the ocean's no place.

Breach of Serenity

I went to the beach for a day of sweet sun,
But the waves had a plan, and oh boy, was it fun!
A friendly old dolphin, all wild and spry,
Took my beach ball and bid me goodbye.

My towel flew high like a flag in a fight,
As seagulls descended, what a comical sight!
They swooped and they squawked, "Not your picnic, dude!"
Chased off my snacks, oh, the flying food feud!

In shallow waves, I narrowly missed,
A crab with a pinch that nobody wished.
He smiled and he scuttled, what a curious chap,
While I danced in the sand, oh how the seasnap!

The tide rolled in fast, like a dog in a race,
And I fled from the surge with a splash on my face.
With laughter and mirth, I returned to my spot,
This beach bum's journey? A giggle? Quite a lot!

The Call of the Abyss

Under the waves, where the fish wear a frown,
I met a grouchy octopus, moody and brown.
He opened his arms, which gave me a fright,
I thought, "Lunch is served!" but it was just a invite.

A clam told a joke, but it was quite shellfish,
In the depths of the ocean, where humor looks selfish.
The crabs shrieked with laughter, whilst spinning about,
'Til the octopus huffed, "Shut it! No clout!"

I tried to swim up, to escape all the jest,
But my snorkel got stuck and I couldn't get blessed!
The lobsters just chuckled, my plight full of charm,
An underwater circus—I'd raise alarm!

So, I wriggled and giggled, through bubbles and brine,
With fish-tales of folly, I felt quite divine.
As the tide pulled me back to the warmth of the sand,
I laughed with the sea; it was more than I planned.

Crashes of Fated Tides

The waves called me forth on a bright summer day,
With buckets and shovels, I set out to play.
But soon with a splosh, I lost sight of my goals,
As a wave came in quick and swallowed my shoals.

My castle of sand, it was grand! It was tall!
Was now just a puddle, oh what a down fall!
My dreams washed away with a fizz and a foam,
While I stood with a laugh, it was time to go home.

The jellyfish danced like a wobbly balloon,
I tried to join in, but it left me marooned.
Swirling and twirling on water and air,
Landing quite goofy, with laughter to share.

Oh creatures of sea, with antics galore,
Awakening dawn at the bright ocean shore.
My and ocean's shared jest, what a raucous delight,
This beach day was pure joy, from sunrise to night!

The Abyss's Embrace

A crab wore a hat, quite the sight,
It danced on the shore in the moonlight.
Fish flashed their fins, with giggles in tow,
While jellyfish jingled, putting on a show.

Seaweed lamented, its party was tossed,
"Why am I here, when I've already lost?"
The clams threw a bash, with pearls on display,
But a seagull swooped down, and stole them away!

A dolphin joked, spinning tales quite absurd,
"I'm a mermaid!" it said, as it wobbled and whirred.
The octopus blushed, long limbs in a tangle,
As it searched for its mates, in a fashionable wrangle.

With laughter that echoed, a chorus of cheer,
The sea roared with joy, as the tides disappeared.
Finny friends frolicked, in a comical race,
In the depths of the blue, where all laughter finds space.

Call of the Remorseful

A whale made a wish, with a flip and a flop,
"Dearest fish, stop asking me to drop!"
Sardines played tag, in a swirling ballet,
While a turtle turned slow, in its own little way.

There once was a shark, with a grin far too broad,
Claimed he was friendly, oh what a facade!
But when he arrived, all the minnows turned gray,
He chased off the laughter, or so they'd say.

Anemones sighed, what a ticklish crew,
They hugged every swimmer, who came drifting through.

But one little clownfish with a boastful finesse,
Giggled and grinned, made an unholy mess.

The sea horses pranced with a regal charm,
While bubble-blowing buddies spread all kinds of balm.
In a wave of mischief, they'd shout, "Let's compete!"
And the call of the remorseful turned into a feat!

Shadows Under Stars

In the moon's silver light, shadows would twirl,
A starfish reached out, gave mischief a whirl.
Gulls cawed with laughter, the night fully bold,
As secrets and giggles in the darkness unfold.

The crabs played hide and go seek on the sand,
"Let's catch those waves!" they said, hand in hand.
But when the tide rolled in with a splashing wee,
The poor little critters brewed cups of sea tea.

A group of fine fish dressed in colorful gear,
Debated the best way to glide without fear.
With every flip-flop, they'd chuckle and tease,
As octopus oversaw, with a flick of the knees.

Then a sneaky old eel gave a wink and a nod,
Turned the night into chaos, oh what a facade!
Underneath starry skies, their laughter fell free,
In the shadows they painted their own jubilee!

Mournful Horizon

A seagull complained, "Oh, the weather's a drag!"
While pebbles conspired, all tied up in a snag.
The ocean just chuckled, its waves all aglow,
As a crab in a tux went off with a show.

Fish in a frenzy, with dreams in their eyes,
Chasing each bubble that floated to rise.
A whale gave a snort, finding humor in plight,
As each wave celebrated the hilarious night.

The sunset turned funky, in hues of bright cheer,
With colors that danced like it had things to clear.
The sand danced along, with its own fancy feet,
As the rolling sea laughed, to their joyous beat.

A pirate fish hummed, with a swagger so bold,
While treasure chest clams shared a story retold.
Though mourning the horizon seemed oh so cliché,
The sea's wit and whimsy would always hold sway.

Cursed Waters

There once was a sailor named Pete,
Whose sea legs were quick on their feet.
With a bottle of grog,
He danced like a frog,
Till he fell in and got quite the greet.

His shipmates all laughed till they cried,
As he splashed and he flailed and he tried.
But the waves had a grudge,
And they wouldn't budge,
So he just floated off with the tide.

With fish that could tickle and tease,
And jellyfish tickling his knees.
He shouted, "Oh dear!
I've no boat, have no fear!
I'll just frolic with dolphins, if you please!

So now he's a legend with fins,
In a sea that plays games - oh, the wins!
His tales never end,
With each wave, a new blend,
Of laughter that bubbles and spins.

The Lure of Lost Fortune

There once was a pirate quite sly,
Who promised each crew a grand high.
With maps full of gold,
He was brazen and bold,
But they found it was just a brown pie.

They sailed to a cursed old isle,
With strange beasts that grinned all the while.
"A treasure!" they said,
Yet found jam instead,
And that pie made them all lose their style.

With pie-fights erupting, oh boy!
They forgot all their plans to enjoy.
The treasure of dough,
Brought laughter in tow,
And left them with crumbs, oh what joy!

So now when they sail out to play,
They laugh at the map light and fey.
For fortune's not gold,
But the tales that unfold,
In sweet, sticky messes each day.

Shimmering Deceptions

In waters where fish love to shine,
Lurks a creature that's rather divine.
With a wink and a grin,
It beckons to win,
But it's really just dinner, I pine!

The seagulls they squawk and they caw,
As they dive at the shimmer, in awe.
But the fish laugh and flee,
From a line, oh so free,
Leaving only a sharp, feathery maw.

A fisherman stood with his bait,
His luck simply couldn't wait.
But the story retold,
Of the fish made of gold,
Was merely a twist of fate!

So he packed up his rod in vain,
While the ocean played tricks with his brain.
He'd catch not a fin,
For the laughs were the win,
And the stories kept him ever sane.

Ink and Salt

A mermaid with ink in her tail,
Used writing to weave her grand tale.
She scribbled at night,
By the moon's silver light,
While the seagulls laughed at her fail.

She wrote of bold pirates and gold,
But forgot the fish tales they told.
With each line a twist,
And a plot they all missed,
Her stories grew stranger, yet bold.

A crab with a quill gave a cheer,
As she conjured up laughter and fear.
With each swipe of ink,
The fish paused to think,
And the waves joined in with a peer.

So she swam with her tales made of salt,
With a grin that could make all hearts halt.
Though no fortune she found,
Her joy knew no bound,
For in laughter, she knew she could vault.

Tidal Whispers

A crab in a tux, with a bowtie so neat,
He dances through foam on the soft sandy sheet.
Seagulls are gossiping, loud as can be,
While fish flip their tails, laughing under the sea.

The surf rolls in laughter, it tickles our toes,
But watch out, the jellyfish lick with a pose!
They float like balloons, but with a sneaky sting,
Turns a beach day fun, into chaos that rings.

A shark tried to smile, with a toothy wide grin,
But tripped on a starfish—oh what a spin!
The tide's got jokes, with waves that jest,
Riptides can chuckle, now isn't that blessed?

So next time you splash, just keep in your mind,
The sea's full of tricks, of a humorous kind.
With laughter in waves, and chuckles in breeze,
It's a whimsical world beneath all the seas!

Lament of Salty Waves

Oh, the waves do wail, with a foamy chagrin,
As they crash on the shores, and pull back again.
Fish gossip about humans, as they wriggle and flop,
Saying, 'Why can't they swim? They keep messing up!'

A sea turtle dreams of a land full of grass,
But trips on a seaweed, covered in sass.
The clams sing soft ballads of pearls gone astray,
While gulls plot their prank—'Let's dive in today!'

The tides twist and turn, in a dance quite absurd,
While octopuses giggle, whispering, 'That's weird!'
The echoes of brine tickle shells on the floor,
As the seaweed shakes hands with a crab at the shore.

Oh salty dear waves, with your puns and your jokes,
You keep us all laughing, even whilst soaking coats.
So raise up your shells, let the laughter resound,
For what lies beneath is the funniest found!

Venom in the Brine

In the depths of the brine where the fun things creep,
A fish wears a tutu, singing to sleep.
But beware of the zesty tang lurking near,
It's not just your sandwich—that's making you leer!

Anemones dance, but they pack quite a punch,
They'll tickle you softly, then ooze with a munch.
A crab with a fiddle plays tunes so off-key,
While jellyfish giggle, flashing glee at the sea.

The sea cucumber's charm is a slippery ploy,
It lures in the foolish, then shrugs with a coy.
While dolphins dive deep, pulling pranks with flair,
Leaving sea urchins gasping in shocked, spiky despair.

So venture with caution through waters that shine,
For laughter and quirk hide dangers benign.
With chuckles that shimmer beneath every line,
In this underwater circus, it's fun that's divine!

Echoes of the Abyss

In the deep, dark abyss, where the octopus plays,
He juggles lost treasures in whimsical ways.
A stingray in shades glides smoothly on by,
While the squid tells a tale that makes neighbors all cry.

A whale's got a playlist so loud, so bizarre,
Singing to fish like a sea-surfing star.
With echoes that shimmer in bubbles of joy,
They dance in a rhythm no human can ploy.

The Anglerfish's lantern, a laugh in disguise,
With a lure so bright, it's a shimmering lie.
But fish laugh it off, in a playful ballet,
As they wiggle away from that one little ray.

So listen, my friend, to the giggles that dwell,
Beneath waves that whisper their shenanigans well.
For in depths of the deep, where the quirky abide,
It's the joy of the ocean, in laughter, we glide!

Nereid's Lament

A mermaid lost her shiny comb,
She dove with glee, but met a gnome.
He stole her trinket, danced with glee,
She chased the laughter, oh, so free.

In bubbles bright, her song she wailed,
As fish about her giggled, hailed.
With every twist and every flip,
She tripped on seaweed, took a dip.

Her fishy friends with laughs in tow,
Played tricks on her, a real show.
She swam in circles, what a plight,
The ocean's mischief, pure delight!

Then, from the depths, a voice declared,
"Your comb's not lost, it's just ensnared!"
With laughter ringing like a bell,
The gnome returned it—oh, what a swell!

Barbs Beneath the Surface

A crab once wore a fancy hat,
He strutted boldly, quite a brat.
But as he danced the tide's sweet tune,
He bumped a fish and lost his rune.

"Oh dear," he said, "what a disgrace!
I'll pinch the sea, and win this race!"
He marched with pride, but then, oh dear,
He slipped on kelp, and drowned in cheer.

The fish all laughed, "You're quite the clown!
With every step, your hat's a frown!"
He caught a wave, and that was that,
The ocean giggled at the brat.

Now crabs, they wear their hats askew,
And dance along, just like the crew.
With barbs and jokes, they roam the tide,
In sea's great humor, they abide!

Currents of Deceit

A jellyfish with tentacles long,
Thought it was right, but oh, so wrong.
She draped a dancer's veil with grace,
But tangled up in seaweed's embrace.

A fish swam by, gave a loud cheer,
"Let go of that! It's not sincere!"
With every twist, the pranks unspooled,
The currents laughed, the jester ruled.

The octopus showed tricks with flair,
Inky clouds formed everywhere.
With legs that waved like ribbons bright,
They pranked the waves, a comical sight!

Yet all was well when dawn arrived,
The jelly learned, she had survived.
With laughter echoing through the sea,
She danced with glee, eternally free!

Harbinger of the Tide

A seagull soared with a great big grin,
He spotted fish, to dive right in!
But as he swooped, he missed his mark,
And landed on a seal, oh hark!

"Watch where you land, you clumsy bird!"
The seal proclaimed, his voice absurd.
With flippers flapping in dismay,
They skidded off into the spray.

The tides conspired, waves did swell,
As laughter roared, they rang a bell.
The seagull cawed, the seal just sighed,
"Next time, friend, let's plan our ride!"

And so they danced through salty foam,
A friendship formed, no need to roam.
Together they'll surf, side by side,
A hilarious pair, the ocean's pride!

Hauntings in the Harbor

Ghosts float on boats, so sly and neat,
Chasing seagulls dancing on their feet.
They whisper jokes of fishy sales,
While dodging nets and slippery trails.

A lantern flickers, a chuckle follows,
As crabs tell tales that quickly swallow.
The moonlight winks with a cheeky grin,
While waves erupt in a giggling spin.

In the still of night, the harbor hums,
With giddy laughter, a tune that thrums.
Old sailors grin as they spin their yarns,
While fish in schools don their best adorns.

Every splash and dive brings forth a joke,
Even the flotsam begins to poke.
Haunting humor fills the salty air,
As ghosts galore put on quite a flair.

In the Wake of Wretchedness

A tale of woe on the water's edge,
Where every wave seems to take a pledge.
Fish crashing boats, oh the sight so bleak,
  Yet giggles erupt amidst the mystique.

Swells whisper secrets of sailors lost,
Each gusty wind, a mischievous frost.
With pirates now laughing instead of brawl,
Their patched eyes twinkling at the squall.

A ship's wooden leg stumbles at sea,
As barnacles giggle, wild and free.
Sailors with tales, they can't stop gaffing,
In the storm's embrace, there's no sign of laughing.

But joy blooms bright through the storm's fierce churn,
Even cold sea tempests can brightly burn.
Where laughter lurks in the heart of strife,
  Funny, how breezes can bring such life.

Cries of the Rockbound

Rocks that jostle, 'Ouch!' they call,
With slippery smiles that enthrall.
Barnacles grumble about their plight,
While waves chuckle in the moonlight.

The gulls caw tales of ships that tripped,
Where laughter erupted, their sails all ripped.
In this jumbled mess, no one feels blue,
As crabs make friends, making do.

Harboring jokes, the tide rolls in,
With chuckles echoing through the din.
For every tumble, there's laughter too,
In the rockbound scene, hilarity is true.

So while the rocks might cry and scream,
The humor flows like a lively stream.
And in their chaos, joy finds its way,
Turning the mishaps to a bright display.

Treacherous Shoals

Oh, the waters shift, a playful jest,
Where boats do dance and fish protest.
Navigating through the wicked trails,
Turning every stumble into tales.

A captain lost, scratching his head,
While sirens sing and the sails turn red.
With every turn, a chuckle flows,
As jellyfish flash their boxed-up prose.

Each wave a riddle, with glee it mocks,
As dolphins leap on the red-clay rocks.
Navigators laugh, despite the fright,
For life's too short to be not polite.

So come with mirth to the treacherous swells,
As laughter rises and the humor tells.
A symphony plays from the shoals that sway,
Turning the chaos into a bright ballet.

Echoes of the Deep

Bubbles rise with giggling sounds,
Fish in tuxedos dance around.
Crabs wear hats, they strut with flair,
An octopus boasts of its new hair.

Seashells chatter, tales to tell,
A clam's a judge; it rings the bell.
Starfish play poker, all in jest,
In the aquatic world, they're the best.

Jellyfish swing with a jelly-like bounce,
Bumping into friends, they laugh and flounce.
A seagull swoops in, joins the fun,
"Oh, I'm not late, I'm just the pun!"

Waves giggle softly on the shore,
Splashes of laughter, who could ask for more?
In this watery realm, joy runs free,
Chasing sunbeams beneath the sea.

Dance of the Salted Waves

Waves do the cha-cha, with splashes so bold,
Seagulls chirping, stories unfold.
Crabs do the twist, while seaweed sways,
And playful dolphins join the frays.

Barnacles gossip, stuck to their rocks,
While snappy shrimp wear fancy frocks.
The lighthouse winks, a friendly sight,
As the tide dances into the night.

Sardines swim in a conga line,
Turtles glide slow, taking their time.
A splash from the back starts a cascade,
Even the sea cucumbers are swayed!

So grab a shell, and let's all groove,
The ocean's rhythm is hard to move.
With laughter echoing on every beat,
Join this salty ballet, it's quite the treat!

Beneath the Surface

The fish have parties in coral caves,
With sea turtles playing, acting like waves.
A sea urchin's juggling, it spills its prize,
"Well, now that's awkward!" a little crab cries.

Anemones tickle each passing fin,
While sardines compete for the biggest grin.
"Don't be shy," says a walrus with flair,
"Come join the fun, we've plenty to share!"

Tangled seaweed hugs a curious whale,
"Oh dear, I'm stuck!" it starts to wail.
Then pufferfish pop with giggles and cheer,
"This party's a blast, let's all stick near!"

Laughter and bubbles rise high in the sea,
Where joy abounds, wild and free.
Under the waves, life is a treat,
With silliness swimming, can't be beat!

Shadows Beneath the Current

In the shadows where the bright fish play,
Lurks Mr. Dabbler, who loves to sway.
"Look at me dance!" he bows with pride,
While schools of minnows take joy in the ride.

The sea floor whispers with secrets untold,
As crabs tell jokes with a pinch of bold.
A flounder confesses, "It's tough to be flat!,"
While starfish giggle, "We're better than that!"

Shadows swirl with a wavy laugh,
As a giant stingray draws up a craft.
"Watch me glide! I'll steal the scene!"
Then flaps of joy burst out, bright and keen.

So join this frolic, beneath the calm,
Where the sea's own humor is wrapped in charm.
In the depths where the silliness flows,
Life becomes a jest where laughter grows!

Sirens' Grief

They sang on rocks, a luring tune,
With fishy breath, they called the moon.
But sailors laughed, their ships would sway,
'These fishy girls won't take us away!'

With hearts so light, they tossed their lines,
For mermaid hair could use some brines.
They whisked away, just for a peek,
But found instead a squawking freak!

The sirens wailed, their hopes now dashed,
As men with nets were finally amassed.
Yet off they swam with a haughty grin,
'See you next tide, we'll always win!'

Maiden's Lament at Dusk

Oh, how I wish a prince would roam,
To rescue me from this wet, cold home.
But crabs just pinch and seagulls laugh,
My dreams of love are a tidal gaff!

Each evening tide brings salty tears,
While barnacles fight my many fears.
My hair's a mess, it tangles wide,
With every wave, my hopes subside.

They tease and tangle, these quarreling waves,
I seek a heart, not crusty knaves.
Yet here I sit, in laughter's grip,
Just me and my sardines on this trip!

Adrift in Mist

A foggy day with no shore in sight,
The captain's hat flew off in fright.
The crew just giggled, they danced around,
While gulls in laughter made funny sounds.

With maps all jumbled, and sails all torn,
We drift in circles, oh how forlorn!
But what's this? A mermaid stands so bold,
'You lost your way? Just follow gold!'

With a wink and a wave, she led the crew,
But only found a big fat shoe.
Dear captain sighed, 'Well, isn't this grand,
We've traded destiny for just one strand!'

Fangs of the Tide

Beneath the waves, there's toothy fun,
Where fishy friends swim, hey look, they run!
With jaws a-jawing and teeth aglow,
They chase their tails, oh what a show!

A shark bumped a seal, oh what a fright,
'It's not a meal! Just past the night!'
They laughed and swirled around the reef,
In finny joy, avoiding grief.

A whale joked loud, 'Help, I've lost my way!'
To fishy fam, it's still a great day!
With fangs and fins, they danced and twirled,
Under the waves, a funny world!

Haunted by the Horizon

Out on the waves, I took a dive,
A fish swam by, wearing a jive.
He winked and grinned, oh what a sight,
I lost my swim trunks, oh what a plight!

Seagulls squawked with a comedic flair,
Stealing my sandwich without a care.
I chased them down, what a silly chase,
Only to trip and fall on my face!

The ocean laughed, with bubbles and foam,
It teased me as if I were its gnome.
With seaweed crown, I came to be,
A king of blunders, proudly at sea!

But as the sun set, I couldn't frown,
For the horizon wore a goofy crown.
With jokes and puns, it lit the way,
To funny tales of a beachcomber's play.

Embrace of the Deep

Beneath the waves where clowns reside,
A crab in a tux looked full of pride.
He danced with seals in a comical spree,
While mermaids giggled at his fancy sea!

The octopus, dressed in eight-legged flare,
Juggled fish with a debonair air.
I tried to join—in my flippers I flopped,
They laughed so hard, I nearly stopped!

A dolphin popped up with a cheeky grin,
He told me jokes, oh where to begin?
With each thump of laughter, I felt so light,
Even the deep seemed friendly tonight!

Though I may have lost my sense of cool,
In depths of delight, I found my pool.
With every splash and goofy twist,
The embrace of the waves I couldn't resist!

Whispers of the Abyss

In the depths where echoes play,
I heard fish gossip in a silly way.
"Did you see how he swam?" a puffer fish said,
"I tried to laugh, I almost turned red!"

An eel with style, all dressed in stripes,
Performed a dance, doing flips and gripes.
I clapped along in a watery trance,
Joining the fun in an awkward dance!

The whispers swirled in a playful tune,
As jellyfish joined in, floating like balloons.
They told tall tales of sailors' glee,
While I just giggled, bobbing in the sea.

But as I twirled in the laughter's embrace,
A wave came crashing, oh what a race!
The whispers faded, but left behind,
A memory of joy, whimsical and kind.

Tides of Sorrow

When the tides rolled in with a gloomy frown,
I slipped on seaweed, plopped head-first down.
The sun was hiding behind a gray shroud,
Even the shells looked a bit too proud!

A crab grumbled, "Hey, don't go too deep,
There's laughter around, but don't fall asleep."
His pinch was firm, but his heart was light,
He cracked the mood, oh what a sight!

Then a wave whispered a riddle in jest,
"Why did the fish cross the sea? To rest!"
The ocean giggled, with bubbles a-burst,
Each drop that fell made it seem like the worst!

But suddenly, a whale sang a tune,
Filled with humor, it chased away gloom.
So while tides may shift, and days feel gray,
Laughter floats up to brightened the way!

Driftwood Dreams

A piece of wood floats by so free,
With a face that looks just like me.
I wave to it, and it grins back,
As we ride together on this watery track.

The seagulls laugh, they dive and swoop,
While we play tag with a big ol' scoop.
A jellyfish floats in, a wobbling guest,
He dances like jelly, but calls it a quest.

Shells join our party, all shapes and sizes,
Some tell tall tales, but all are surprises.
We laugh till we cry, forgetting our woes,
As the stars twinkle down on our driftwood toes.

So here's to the friends that float on the tide,
With wood, waves, and giggles, we take it in stride.
In this salty ocean, with dreams that gleam,
We'll drift ever onward, in shared silly dreams.

Howl of the Riptide

A wave howls loud like a laugh in the night,
Grabbing swimmers for a silly fright.
They're tossed and they're turned, a swirling ballet,
"Help! I'm doing the backstroke!" they yell, "Not today!"

The tide tugs hard, a slippery game,
Pulling in fish with a luring name.
"Come closer," it whispers, "We'll dance on the sand!"
"Forget your woes, take my slimy hand!"

But if you're brave and bold enough,
To conquer the waves that are often rough,
You'll find a treasure of laughter and glee,
In every splash: "Hey, you got me!"

So ride the wild waves, embrace the froth,
While giggles and splashes mark the path that you troth.
For every wave's howl is just a big joke,
That brings us together with every soak.

The Tide's Grief

The ocean weeps, but wait, what's that?
A fish wearing boots and a squishy hat!
It flops and it flounders, doing a jig,
While seaweed twirls around like a big green wig.

A crab in a suit starts a comedy show,
"Why did the clam take the fish for a row?"
He gestures wildly, his claws all a-flail,
As the ocean giggles with its bubbly tale.

The tide takes a breath and lets out a chuckle,
As shells whisper secrets, it's more than a huddle.
"Don't cry," says the wave, "it's all part of the fun,
Just look at the starfish, they're out for a run!"

So when the seas weep, just dance on the shore,
Join the salty jesters and ask for some more.
For laughter and waves, they share the same beat,
A tide that rumbles has room for your feet.

Eclipsed by Waves

The moon peeks down with a funny face,
While waves crash on shores like a wild embrace.
They tickle the toes of those on the sand,
"We're just here for fun, won't you understand?"

A sea turtle slides with a wink and a grin,
Challenging fish to a whimsical spin.
"Bet you can't catch me; I'm slick as can be!"
While dolphins jump high, saying, "Look at me!"

Shells whisper secrets, in hushes and laughs,
As barnacles join in for silly old chaffs.
The waves roll on in a most comedic rhyme,
Calling all folks to prove they're in time.

So dance with the sea and the stars up above,
Let waves take your worries; just swim like a dove.
For laughter's the tide that unifies all,
Embrace every splash, answer the ocean's call.

Saltwater Shadows

In a boat with my buddy, we found some old bait,
He said, "This will work!" I said, "Hold your hate!"
The fish swam around us, they laughed like a joke,
While we tangled our lines, oh what a hoax!

A crab took a snap; I thought it was fame,
But it chomped on my toe, just not part of the game.
With nets in a tangle, we lost the whole day,
Came home with a story, our pride in dismay.

The seagulls caught wind and they joined in the mess,
As we spilled our lunch and they thought it was best.
One stole my sandwich, he took flight with glee,
While I shook my fist, shouting curses at sea.

We laughed until sunset, our spirits were bright,
Even when the fish grinned, we knew they were right.
With salt in our hair, and a smile really wide,
It's clear that the ocean's a fun-loving guide.

Nautical Nightmares

Sailing through waters where the jellyfish float,
I slipped on the deck and went right down the throat!
I surfaced with bubbles, and wiggly things too,
Those nightmares in blue turned my laughter askew.

The compass was spinning; I'm sure it's possessed,
Pointing at ice cream, like it really knows best.
The waves kept on chuckling, they tossed us about,
While I tried to navigate and scream out for help!

I found a lost shoe, just floating along,
It begged me for rescue, a real life's wronged song.
It danced with the dolphins, who mocked with delight,
Made me question if sailing was dumb or just bright.

As the sun started dipping, we tossed back a drink,
Picturing mermaids and their silly pink bling.
In the end we were grateful, we didn't get lost,
Just giggles and tales, but what a fun cost!

The Dark Kiss of Ocean's Breath

A wave came a-rolling, it looked quite bizarre,
Saying, "Hello, friends! Where's your sailor's car?"
We laughed till we farted, oh, what a surprise,
That breath from the ocean, it smelled like old fries!

A fish came a-flopping, right into my lap,
He grinned like a cat, said, "Welcome to my map!"
I asked him for directions, but he swam away,
Just blowing a bubble and calling it a day.

The seaweed was dancing, quite loud in the brine,
It tangled my limbs and said, "You're looking fine!"
With a wink and a curl, it pulled me along,
Till I realized I'd just joined its seaweed throng.

As night fell upon us, we toasted the sea,
To shadows and fish with a glass full of glee.
With a kiss from the ocean, we let out a cheer,
Laughing at the antics and light-hearted fears.

Dangers in the Deep Blue

My buddy swam first; he thought it was grand,
Until a sea cucumber slipped from his hand.
It wobbled and jiggled, right over his head,
While he twirled in a panic, he wish he'd stayed dead!

The octopus grinned, he wore quite a crown,
Said, "Dude, don't you know? You look silly, not brown!"

We giggled and struggled, two clowns in the tide,
As clams took our picture, with shells open wide.

With barnacles pinching, they stole our cool hats,
And started a fashion parade with some rats.
The currents were chuckling, they knew we were stuck,
In a swirling catastrophe, oh, what bad luck!

But as the tide turned, we gave one last roar,
With the jellyfish joining, we danced on the shore.
For dangers in blue often lead to good cheer,
And that's how we ended our wild water year!

www.ingramcontent.com/pod-product-compliance
Lightning Source LLC
Chambersburg PA
CBHW070322120526
44590CB00017B/2790